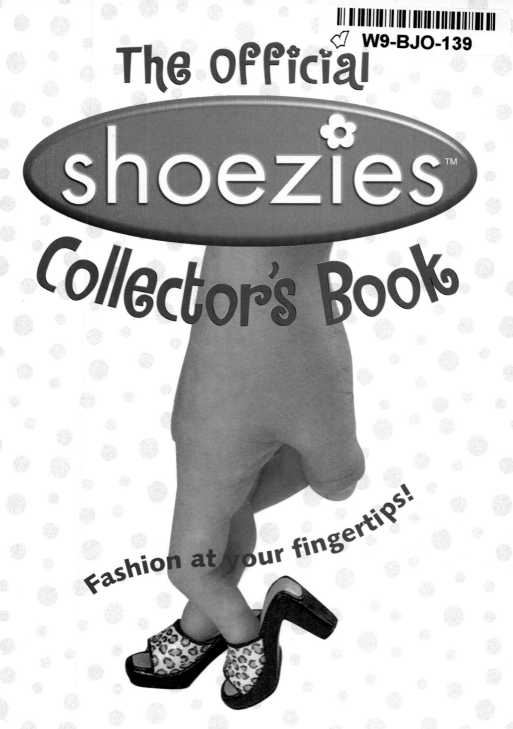

The Official

shoezies™

Collector's Book

Fashion at your fingertips!

SCHOLASTIC INC.

New York   Toronto   London   Auckland   Sydney
Mexico City   New Delhi   Hong Kong   Buenos Aires

W9-BJO-139

ISBN: 0-439-37067-1

© 2001 Hasbro, Inc.

Design by Louise Bova

SHOEZIES™ is a trademark of Hasbro, Inc. All rights reserved. Published by Scholastic Inc.

SCHOLASTIC and associated logos are trademarks and/or registered trademarks of Scholastic Inc.

12 11 10 9 8 7 6 5 4 3 2   1 2 3 4 5 6/0

Printed in the U.S.A.
First Scholastic printing, October 2001

What do Dorothy and the Greek god Mercury have in common? Great shoes! Dorothy's ruby slippers sent her back over the rainbow, and Mercury's winged sandals helped him run heavenly errands for the gods of Mount Olympus.

Shoes have a long history. The earliest shoes can be traced back to Native Americans living in Missouri in 8,000 B.C. But shoes have had many uses other than protecting feet. Instead of stockings, children used to leave their shoes out on Christmas Eve to be filled with presents. In ancient Greece, shoes were used to separate citizens from slaves. Since shoes were considered a sign of social status, slaves had to remain barefoot.

Thousands of years later, shoes are still a very important part of everyday life. What's the finishing touch to any outfit? The perfect pair of shoes! Today's top fashion designers compete to create the newest, hottest shoe designs, and now keeping up with the trends has never been easier. Introducing SHOEZIES, the fashion-forward footwear brand for your fingers! If you can't wait to collect all of your favorite shoe fashions, then this is the book for you. It's the only guide you'll need to the fantastic world of SHOEZIES. Inside you'll find need-to-know trivia, intriguing shoe legends and superstitions, and exciting shoe facts!

If you think you've mastered all the SHOEZIES mania, take a look at the excellent do-it-yourself tips, and turn any old shoe into a fashion phenomenon! Now you can design, create, and collect some of the coolest shoe fashions to hit the streets!

FOOTNOTES

Let's start with a few fabulous facts about footwear:

 The word "shoe" comes from the Anglo-Saxon word *sceo* meaning "to cover."

 The sandal is the oldest shoe in existence.

 The patron saint of shoemakers is St. Crispin, who was born in the third century A.D. He became a shoemaker, and October 25 is celebrated as St. Crispin's Day and the Shoemaker's Holiday.

 Romans were first to cut shoes for the left and right foot.

 The average American woman owns 30 pairs of shoes . . . how many do you own?

 During the Middle Ages, the pointed toes of shoes were often so long that they had to be held off the ground with fine chains or ribbons tied around the knee.

 The average person walks 2,000 miles a year.

 Egyptians and Romans drew the faces of their enemies on the soles of their sandals so they could literally step on them.

In 200 A.D., the Roman Emperor Aurelius issued a decree that only he and his successors could wear red sandals.

Where did the word "sneaker" come from? Well, when canvas shoes with rubber soles were first introduced in the 1800s, sneak thieves quickly realized that they could move around quietly in these shoes and thus the name "sneakers" was born.

Heels on shoes were considered a sign of nobility because of the Mongol horsemen who had bright red wooden heels on their boots. Since owning a horse was expensive, riders and high heels became identified with nobility. We still say that someone is "well-heeled" if he or she is wealthy.

In 15th-century England, men wore shoes called "duckbills" because the toes looked like a duck's bill. A law was passed decreeing that the shoes could be no wider than five-and-one-half inches.

In Japan, people wear *geta*. Geta have a flat wood sole, a "V"-style toe thong, and are raised up on two thin, wood blocks. In Japanese the strips are called *ha*, which is the Japanese word for tooth or teeth. These "ha" can be two inches tall—or more!

Keds were first mass-marketed as canvas-top "sneakers" in 1917. These were the first popular sneakers and the first tennis shoes.

In 1917 the high-top sneaker for basketball was introduced by Converse. It was called the Converse All Stars.

Thigh-high boots were first worn by pirates. The term "bootlegging" comes from their habit of hiding valuables, or "booty," inside their boots.

Wooden shoes have been worn for centuries throughout Europe. They are still being worn in the lowlands, the Netherlands, because of the soggy soil.

Nike has sold nearly 100 million pairs of Michael Jordan's Air Jordan shoes.

The record for the biggest feet in the world is currently held by a man in the United States who wears U.S. size 28.5 shoes.

The most expensive shoes ever were commissioned by Emperor Bokassa of the Central African Empire (now Republic) for his coronation on December 4, 1977. Made by the House of Beluti in France, the pearl-studded shoes cost $85,000.

For a fashion show in 1999, Manolo Blahnik made six pairs of gold shoes with 18-karat-covered heels and front bands. The shoes cost approximately $9,944 each, and were protected by bodyguards during the show.

When she left the Philippines to go into exile in Hawaii in 1986, Imelda Marcos—wife of the former dictator—left behind 1,220 pairs of shoes.

There is a museum that celebrates footwear and shoemaking. The Bata Shoe Museum in Toronto, Canada, has over 10,000 items that span 4,500 years.

Twenty-five percent of all the bones in the human body are found in the foot.

The human foot has 18 muscles.

There were eight pairs of ruby slippers made for *The Wizard of Oz*. The last pair sold at auction for $165,000.

In the mid-1500's women began wearing shoes known as *chopines*. These shoes had a platform base that could make a woman look taller—often by as much as 24 inches! Because walking in them was so difficult, women often walked with canes or an escort to support them.

SOLE SPECIFIC

While a lot of shoes are designed simply to be fashionable, some shoes were created for a specific purpose. Here is a look at some shoes that have function as well as fashion:

Athletic Shoes:

Spiked shoes for running were developed in 1852, and by 1894 the Spalding Company offered three different kinds of running shoes. The first sports shoe company was founded by Joseph William Foster in the 1890s. That company eventually became Reebok. However, the inventor of the modern running shoe was Adolf Dassler, who began making running shoes in 1920. In 1948, Dassler founded his own company—Adidas.

Tap Shoes:

Tap shoes actually started out as clogs. In Victorian England, clog dancing was popular with the working classes. Dancers used to tap their wooden clogs on the stone streets to create rhythms. When clog dancing came to America in the 19th century, it was transformed into tap dancing. Tap shoes have metal pieces called jingles on their soles. These jingles make a "tapping" sound when the shoe strikes the ground.

Cowboy Boots:

The cowboy boot is based on the Wellington boot, named after the English Duke of Wellington—the man who defeated Napoleon. The original cowboy boot was a low-heeled, round-toed work boot, but then Hollywood started making Westerns. Actual cowboy boots were just too boring for movies so Hollywood added fancy stitching, cutouts, and inlays to the boots to make them more interesting. Today's cowboy boots are really fantasy footwear created by Hollywood and have almost no connection to the Wild West.

Space Boots:

When the astronauts went walking on the moon, they wore special overshoes that slipped over the boots in their space suits. The outer layer of the shoes was made from a metal-woven fabric while the sole was made of ribbed silicone rubber.

Ballet Pointe Shoes:

The shoes that ballerinas wear when they dance on their toes are called pointe shoes. The shoe is a soft-satin-covered slipper with a hard toe that supports the weight of the dancer. The toe box of the pointe shoe is made of layers of burlap and paper, saturated with glue. The shank or midsole is usually made from some form of paper such as cardboard or fiberboard. Most pointe shoes will fit either foot—there is no left and right shoe.

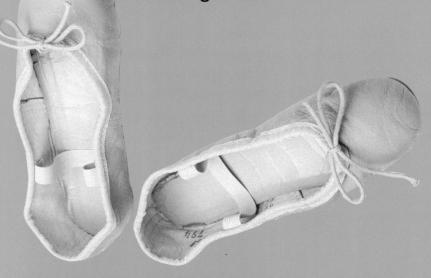

MINI GOES MAXI

Here are all 24 **SHOEZIES** styles close up and ready for you to fill in lots of fabulous **SHOEZIES** facts! Which of your favorite stars would wear this pair of **SHOEZIES**? Maybe it's your best friend or your favorite singer or movie star. You decide whose feet would look fabulous in these **SHOEZIES**. And what about you? Would you wear them? What outfit would you wear with them? And where would your **SHOEZIES** take you? It could be to the beach, or a concert, or the mall, or a totally happening party. It's time to let your imagination take a walk, so grab a pen or a pencil and get ready.

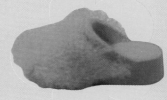

Girl's Night Out

Hot Pink Leopard

When I got this pair: _____

What I'd wear with this pair: _____

_____

Where I'd wear this pair: _____

_____

Which of my friends would wear this pair: _____

Which celebrity would wear this pair: _____

Totally Tulips

When I got this pair: _____

What I'd wear with this pair: _____

_____

Where I'd wear this pair: _____

_____

Which of my friends would wear this pair: _____

Which celebrity would wear this pair: _____

Plum Pretty

When I got this pair: _____

What I'd wear with this pair: _____

_____

Where I'd wear this pair: _____

_____

Which of my friends would wear this pair: _____

Which celebrity would wear this pair: _____

Shake n' Shimmer

When I got this pair: _____

What I'd wear with this pair: _____

_____

Where I'd wear this pair: _____

_____

Which of my friends would wear this pair: _____

Which celebrity would wear this pair: _____

Sneak Peeps

When I got this pair: _____

What I'd wear with this pair: _____

_____

Where I'd wear this pair: _____

_____

Which of my friends would wear this pair: _____

Which celebrity would wear this pair: _____

Funkin' Fimmies

When I got this pair: _____

What I'd wear with this pair: _____

_____

Where I'd wear this pair: _____

_____

Which of my friends would wear this pair: _____

Which celebrity would wear this pair: _____

steppin' Lively

Skylark

When I got this pair: _____

What I'd wear with this pair: _____

_____

Where I'd wear this pair: _____

_____

Which of my friends would wear this pair: _____

Which celebrity would wear this pair: _____

Blueberry Pie

When I got this pair: _____

What I'd wear with this pair: _____

_____

Where I'd wear this pair: _____

_____

Which of my friends would wear this pair: _____

Which celebrity would wear this pair: _____

Wicker Cool

When I got this pair: _____

What I'd wear with this pair: _____

_____

Where I'd wear this pair: _____

_____

Which of my friends would wear this pair: _____

Which celebrity would wear this pair: _____

When I got this pair: _____

What I'd wear with this pair: _____

_____

Where I'd wear this pair: _____

_____

Which of my friends would wear this pair: _____

Which celebrity would wear this pair: _____

On The Moove

When I got this pair: _____

What I'd wear with this pair: _____

_____

Where I'd wear this pair: _____

_____

Which of my friends would wear this pair: _____

Which celebrity would wear this pair: _____

When I got this pair: _____

What I'd wear with this pair: _____

_____

Where I'd wear this pair: _____

_____

Which of my friends would wear this pair: _____

Which celebrity would wear this pair: _____

She's Got Style

When I got this pair: _____

What I'd wear with this pair: _____

_____

Where I'd wear this pair: _____

_____

Which of my friends would wear this pair: _____

Which celebrity would wear this pair: _____

Clean Sweep

When I got this pair: _____

What I'd wear with this pair: _____

_____

Where I'd wear this pair: _____

_____

Which of my friends would wear this pair: _____

Which celebrity would wear this pair: _____

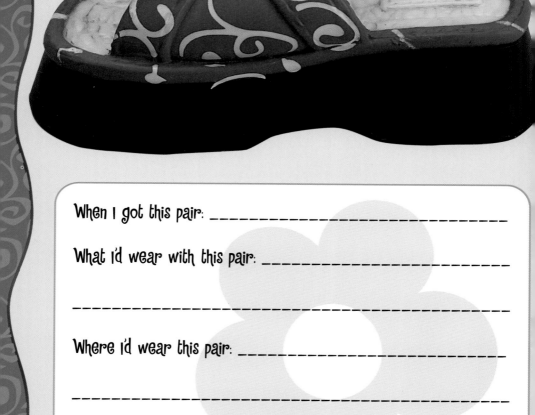

Cosmic Curls

When I got this pair: _____

What I'd wear with this pair: _____

_____

Where I'd wear this pair: _____

_____

Which of my friends would wear this pair: _____

Which celebrity would wear this pair: _____

O'Mary Max

When I got this pair: _____

What I'd wear with this pair: _____

_____

Where I'd wear this pair: _____

_____

Which of my friends would wear this pair: _____

Which celebrity would wear this pair: _____

Sunflower Fun

When I got this pair: _____

What I'd wear with this pair: _____

_____

Where I'd wear this pair: _____

_____

Which of my friends would wear this pair: _____

Which celebrity would wear this pair: _____

Velvet Kicks

When I got this pair: _____

What I'd wear with this pair: _____

_____

Where I'd wear this pair: _____

_____

Which of my friends would wear this pair: _____

Which celebrity would wear this pair: _____

Big Night Out

When I got this pair: _____

What I'd wear with this pair: _____

_____

Where I'd wear this pair: _____

_____

Which of my friends would wear this pair: _____

Which celebrity would wear this pair: _____

When I got this pair: _____

What I'd wear with this pair: _____

_____

Where I'd wear this pair: _____

_____

Which of my friends would wear this pair: _____

Which celebrity would wear this pair: _____

When I got this pair: _____

What I'd wear with this pair: _____

_____

Where I'd wear this pair: _____

_____

Which of my friends would wear this pair: _____

Which celebrity would wear this pair: _____

When I got this pair: _____

What I'd wear with this pair: _____

_____

Where I'd wear this pair: _____

_____

Which of my friends would wear this pair: _____

Which celebrity would wear this pair: _____

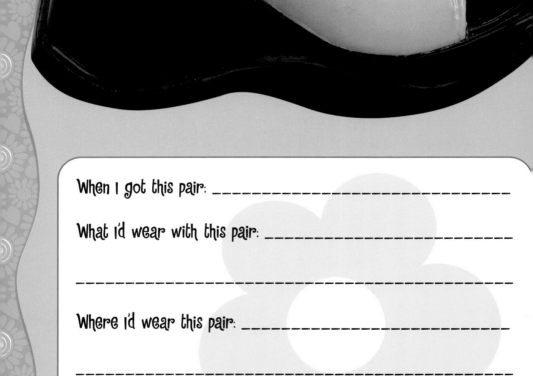

Whisper Wedge

When I got this pair: _____

What I'd wear with this pair: _____

_____

Where I'd wear this pair: _____

_____

Which of my friends would wear this pair: _____

Which celebrity would wear this pair: _____

Pixie Doodles

When I got this pair: _____

What I'd wear with this pair: _____

_____

Where I'd wear this pair: _____

_____

Which of my friends would wear this pair: _____

Which celebrity would wear this pair: _____

SHOE-PERSTITIONS

Good-luck shoes:

 From the Middle Ages, shoes have been considered lucky. This may be because shoes were expensive and it was common practice to leave your shoes to a family member in your will. The saying "Following in your father's footsteps" may have arisen from this custom.

 As late as the 19th century, old shoes were left in the roofs of houses to keep away evil spirits.

 Throwing shoes after someone who is going on a journey was supposed to bring them good luck.

 An old Scottish tale states that when you throw a shoe over a house and then look to see which way the toe of the shoe points when it reaches the ground, you will see the direction you are destined to travel before too long.

 Tying old shoes to a newlywed's car is supposed to bring the bride and groom good luck as well as chase away evil.

 Squeaky shoes were considered a sign of good luck.

Some people put salt and pepper in their left boot for good luck.

People with holes in the soles of their shoes were destined to become wealthy.

Bad-luck shoes:

Shoes placed on a table are thought to be a bad omen and will cause a quarrel in the house.

It is bad luck if a beetle crawls out of your shoe.

Never place shoes over your head or keep shoes under the bed—both are bad luck.

Actors never put shoes on a chair in their dressing rooms because it is considered bad luck.

It's a bad omen to place your left foot on the ground first thing in the morning or to put on your left shoe first.

Walking around with one shoe on and the other off will bring bad luck for a year.

U DO THE SHOE

Be your own shoe designer! The following pages are filled with shoe styles for you to decorate. Now is your chance to make the perfect **SHOEZIES** collection. Don't forget to name your sassy styles!

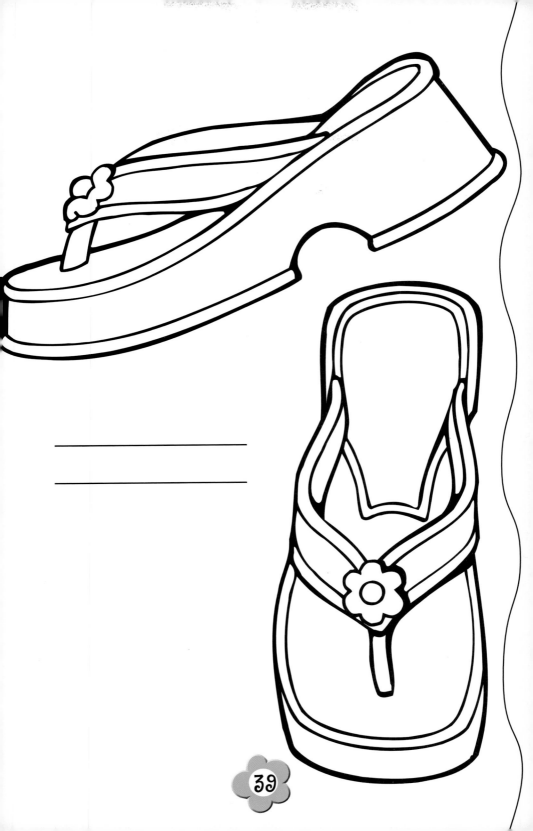

39

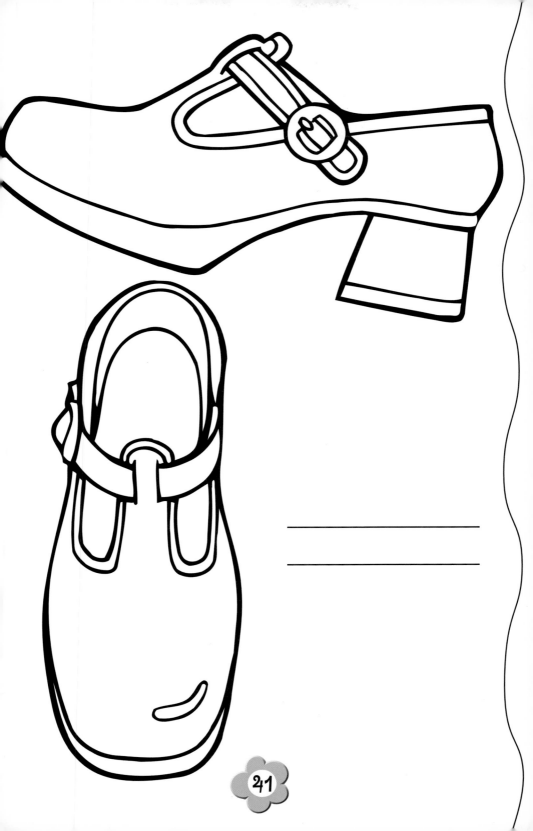

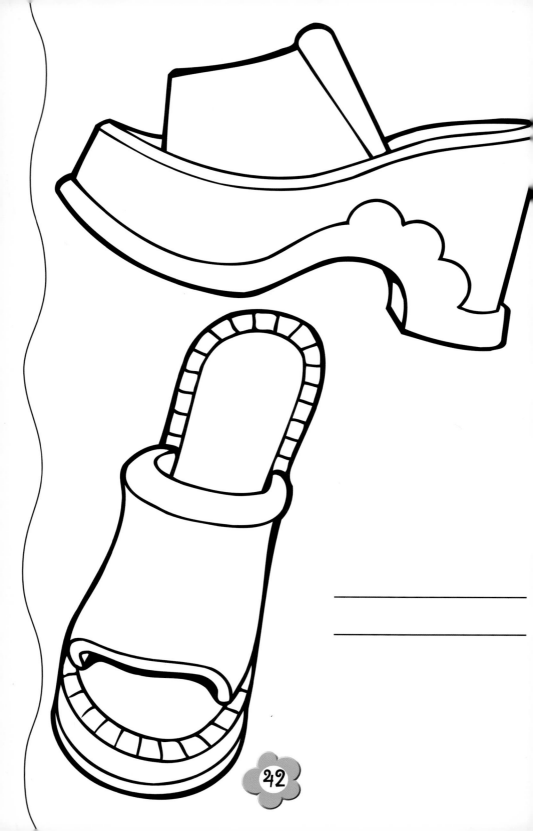

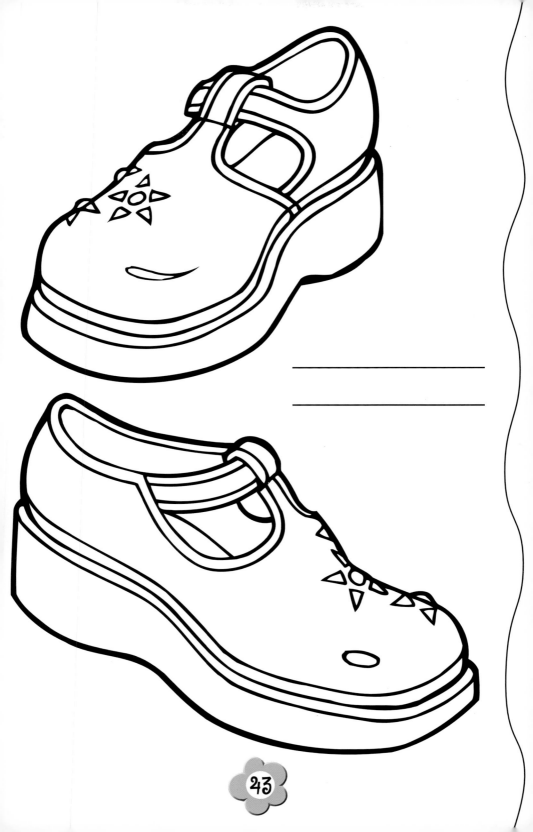

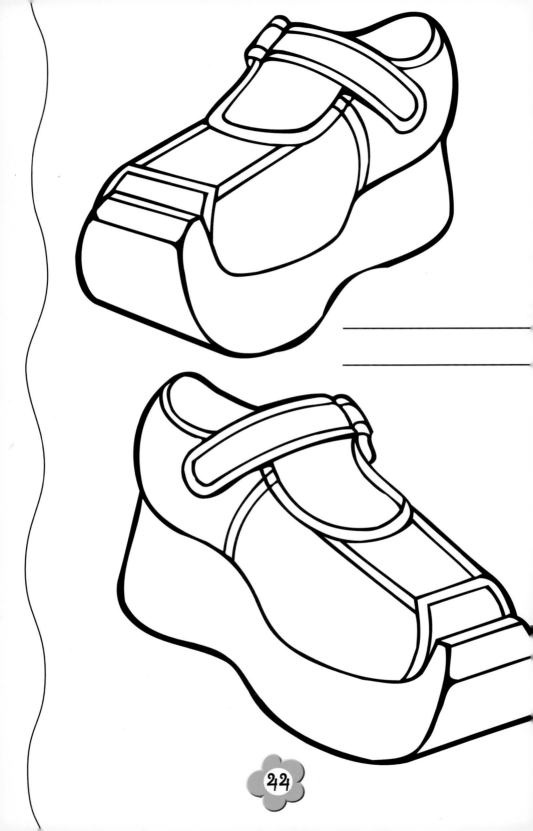

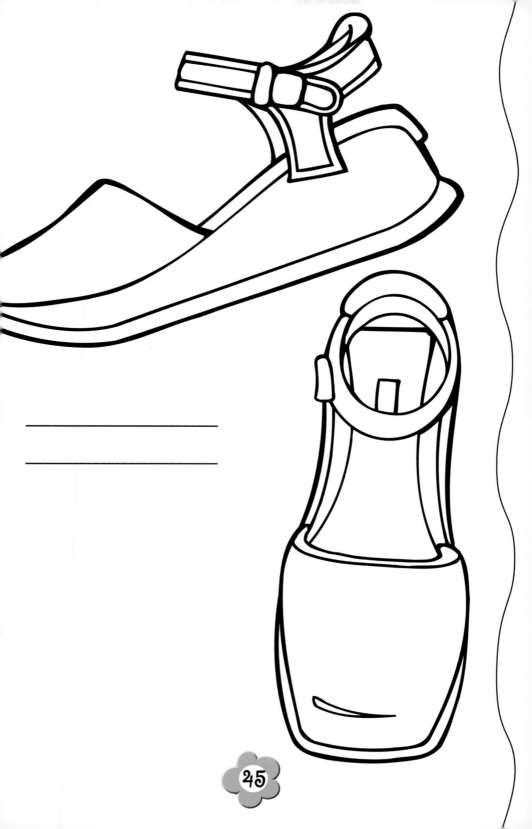

45

D.I.Y.

Do it yourself. Now that you're an experienced shoe designer, it's time to use your talents to dress up your real shoes. Here are a few ideas for you to try—but remember to ask your parents for permission before you start!

Turn your favorite sneakers into something special by decorating the laces. Here are some suggestions:

Markers
Use permanent markers to turn white shoelaces into colorful keepsakes.

Ribbons
Use colorful or lacy ribbons instead of regular shoelaces to give your sneakers a new look.

Beads
Give your shoes a kick by threading beads onto your shoelaces for added color. You could even add small bells so that everyone can hear you coming.

You can decorate your other shoes as well:

Wooden heels
Add some design and color to the wooden heels of your clogs, slip-ons, or sandals. Use acrylic paint to create designs and patterns. Or with glue and rhinestone create some designs that sparkle.

Funky Flip-Flops
Decorate your flip-flops with cloth wrapped around the straps. Then add satin bows, beads, or rhinestones to the cloth, or just glue a big fake flower in the middle for some flower power.

Shoe Your Knowledge

How well do you know shoes? See if you can figure out the following bits of shoe trivia (answers are on page 48).

1. Which performer from Graceland sang about his "Blue Suede Shoes"?

2. Who wore a pair of winged sandals?

3. What was the name of the first type of basketball high-tops?

4. Which careless girl lost a glass slipper at a dance?

5. Who clicked the heels of her ruby slippers so she could go home?

6. What was the name of the movie about a ballerina who couldn't stop dancing?

7. Who had so many children she didn't know what to do?

8. Which animal wears shoes?

9. Where can you find the most famous footprints in Hollywood?

10. What color are Mickey Mouse's shoes?

11. Which fairy tale was about a group of sisters who wore out a pair of shoes every night?

12. What type of shoes did thieves like to wear?

13. Which fairy tale featured a talking cat that liked to wear boots?

14. How many shoes does the entire cast of the Radio City Music Hall Christmas Spectacular go through in a day?

15. What do you call tap dancing with no music?

ANSWERS TO QUIZ

1. Elvis Presley
2. Mercury, the winged messenger of the Greek gods
3. Converse All Stars
4. Cinderella
5. Dorothy in *The Wizard of Oz*
6. *The Red Shoes*
7. The old woman who lived in a shoe
8. Horses
9. Mann's Chinese Theater
10. Yellow
11. "The Twelve Dancing Princesses"
12. Sneakers
13. "Puss in Boots"
14. 500 pairs
15. Tacit